Saints and Sinners: The Untold Stories of Abuse in the catholic church

Sophia Fairview

Published by Independent Artists Network, 2024.

While every precaution has been taken in the preparation of this book, the publisher assumes no responsibility for errors or omissions, or for damages resulting from the use of the information contained herein.

SAINTS AND SINNERS: THE UNTOLD STORIES OF ABUSE IN THE CATHOLIC CHURCH

First edition. January 1, 2024.

Copyright © 2024 Sophia Fairview.

ISBN: 979-8223585916

Written by Sophia Fairview.

Table of Contents

"The Veiled Sins: A Chronicle of Abuse in the Catholic Church"

The Origins of the Catholic Church's Power

The early days of the Catholic Church and its rise to power in society.

The Catholic Church has a long and storied history, dating back to its origins in the first century AD. It all began with Jesus Christ, whom the Church believes to be the son of God and the founder of their faith. After his crucifixion and resurrection, his disciples carried on his teachings and formed the foundation of what would become the Catholic Church.

In the early days, the Church faced persecution and hardship, yet it persevered and grew in number. It gained followers through its message of salvation and eternal life through faith in Christ. As the Church expanded, it began to have a profound influence on society, shaping the lives of millions of people across the world. This influence stemmed from a combination of factors, including the Church's theological foundations, its hierarchical structure, and its involvement in politics.

With its teachings based on the scriptures and traditions of Christianity, the Catholic Church became a source of guidance and moral authority for believers. Its doctrines, such as the divinity of Christ and the sacraments, formed the bedrock of the Church's teachings and provided a framework for understanding and living a Christian life. By emphasizing the importance of faith and salvation, the Church offered a path to redemption and spiritual fulfillment to its followers.

Furthermore, the spread of the Church's influence can be attributed to its ability to adapt and assimilate into different cultures and regions. As it expanded, the Church incorporated local customs and traditions, making it accessible to people of diverse backgrounds. This inclusiveness allowed the Church to connect with individuals on a personal level, fostering a sense of belonging and community.

One cannot overlook the hierarchical structure of the Church as a key factor in its rise to power. The Pope, who is believed to be the successor of Saint Peter, holds a central role in the Church's governance and decision-making. Underneath the Pope are bishops, priests, and other clergy members who play vital roles in leading worship, administering sacraments, and providing guidance to their respective communities.

Additionally, the Church's involvement in politics played a significant role in shaping the course of history. Throughout the centuries, popes and the Catholic Church found themselves in positions of influence and power. They often acted as advisors to kings and emperors, mediating conflicts, and even exercising temporal authority. This intertwining of religious and political power lent credibility and clout to the Church, further solidifying its grip on society.

Nevertheless, the early Church was not without its controversies and criticisms. From the division between the Eastern Orthodox Church and the Roman Catholic Church to the corruption and excesses of the medieval papacy, the Church's actions and policies were often subject to scrutiny. These early criticisms would foreshadow the challenges that the Catholic Church would face in the centuries to come.

As we delve deeper into the history of the Catholic Church, it becomes apparent how its rise to power and influence laid the foundation for the complex issues that would later plague it. The journey from its humble beginnings to its position as a global religious institution would shape not only the Church itself but also the course of history and the lives of countless individuals.

The theological foundations of the Catholic Church and its influence on believers.

At the core of the Catholic Church's power lies its theological foundations, which provide the framework for belief and practice. These doctrinal principles have shaped the lives of believers and continue to guide the Church's teachings and rituals.

Central to Catholic theology is the belief in the Holy Trinity - God the Father, God the Son (Jesus Christ), and God the Holy Spirit. This concept of the Trinity underscores the divine nature of the Church's teachings and the interconnectedness of God's presence in the world.

The Church places a strong emphasis on the sacraments, which are sacred rituals through which believers can receive God's grace. These sacraments include baptism, confirmation, Eucharist, reconciliation, anointing of the sick, holy orders, and matrimony. Each sacrament serves a unique purpose, such as initiation into the Church, forgiveness of sins, and the reception of the body and blood of Christ. Through the sacraments, Catholics encounter the divine and experience a deep connection with the Church community.

Moreover, the Catholic Church places great importance on Scripture and tradition as sources of authority. The Bible, which contains the Old and New Testaments, is considered the inspired Word of God. The Church interprets and teaches from the Scriptures, guiding believers on matters of faith and morality. In addition to Scripture, the Church also draws from the richness of its traditions, including the writings of early Church fathers, papal encyclicals, and councils.

The teachings of the Catholic Church provide a moral compass for believers, addressing various aspects of life, from personal ethics to social justice. The Church's teachings on issues such as abortion, homosexuality, and euthanasia have been topics of great controversy and debate. These moral teachings have often influenced public opinion and shaped societal norms.

By offering a comprehensive framework for faith and practice, the Catholic Church has the power to inspire and transform the lives of its followers. Through the guidance of the Church's teachings, believers are encouraged to live out their faith in the world, seeking to follow Christ's example of love, compassion, and justice. This influence extends beyond religious practices and has an impact on the way Catholics navigate their personal and professional lives.

The theological foundations of the Catholic Church are not only a source of spiritual guidance for believers but also a source of authority and power for the institution itself. These doctrines and teachings have provided the basis for the Church's influence on individuals, communities, and societies throughout history. However, as we explore further, we will uncover how the abuse crisis within the Catholic Church has challenged these foundations and tested the faith of its followers.

The spread of the Church's influence across different regions and cultures.

One remarkable aspect of the Catholic Church's history is its ability to spread its influence across diverse regions and cultures. From its humble beginnings in Jerusalem, the Church expanded its reach, transcending geographic boundaries and adapting to local customs and traditions.

The early missionaries, driven by their faith and zeal, played a crucial role in the Church's expansion. They embarked on journeys to remote lands, bringing the message of Christianity to new territories. These missionaries encountered diverse cultures and languages, and in their efforts to spread the Gospel, they often incorporated local customs and traditions into Catholic practices. By embracing cultural diversity, the Church established deeper connections with individuals and communities, making Christianity more accessible and relatable.

Over time, the Church became a unifying force, providing a sense of identity and community for its followers. In regions that were already under a dominant religious or cultural influence, the Catholic Church found ways to coexist and integrate aspects of the local culture into its practices. This approach not only facilitated the conversion of people but also enabled the Church to establish a foothold within different societies.

As the Church expanded its influence, it also encountered challenges and conflicts. In some cases, the spread of Catholicism was met with resistance, particularly in regions where other religious traditions were deeply rooted. Tensions arose as the Church sought to assert its authority and convert believers from existing faiths. These clashes often resulted in religious conflicts and the blending of indigenous practices with Catholic rituals in syncretic forms of worship.

Despite these challenges, the Catholic Church's adaptability and flexibility played a significant role in its successful spread. The Church's ability to bridge cultural divides, incorporate local customs, and adapt to different languages helped it forge connections with diverse populations. These connections allowed Catholicism to take root and flourish, creating a sense of belonging and community among the faithful.

Today, the Catholic Church is a truly global institution, with a presence in almost every corner of the world. Its followers span various races, ethnicities, and cultures, forming a diverse and vibrant community. The spread of the Church's influence across different regions and cultures has not only strengthened its position as a religious institution but has also contributed to its rich heritage and global impact.

The hierarchical structure of the Church and its role in maintaining control.

The Catholic Church operates with a hierarchical structure that has been fundamental to its organization and governance throughout history. This hierarchical system, with the Pope at its apex, serves as a mechanism for maintaining control and ensuring the preservation of the Church's teachings and traditions.

At the top of the hierarchical structure is the Pope, who is considered the successor of Saint Peter and holds the highest authority within the Church. The Pope is believed to possess the power of infallibility, meaning that when speaking on matters of faith and doctrine, his pronouncements are considered to be without error. The Pope is not only the spiritual leader of the Church but also its temporal head, responsible for making important decisions and representing the Church on a global scale.

Beneath the Pope are the bishops, who oversee specific regions or dioceses within the Church. These bishops are appointed by the Pope and are responsible for the spiritual and administrative affairs of their respective regions. They preside over local churches, ordain priests, and ensure that Church teachings are upheld within their jurisdiction.

Next in the hierarchy are the priests, who serve as spiritual leaders within individual parishes. They are responsible for conducting religious services, administering sacraments, and providing pastoral care to their congregations. The priests act as intermediaries between God and the faithful, guiding them in matters of faith, morality, and religious practice.

The hierarchical structure of the Church serves several purposes. First and foremost, it acts as a means of maintaining orthodoxy and the consistent transmission of Church teachings. The Pope, bishops, and priests are responsible for interpreting and disseminating the doctrines and traditions of the Church to the faithful. This hierarchical structure ensures that the teachings of the Church remain unified and consistent across different regions and cultures.

Additionally, the hierarchical structure of the Church allows for efficient decision-making and the implementation of Church policies. Through the clear chain of command, the Church can respond to changes in society and address challenges that arise. This hierarchical framework facilitates collaboration and coordination among various levels of leadership within the Church, enabling it to adapt and navigate the complexities of the modern world.

However, the hierarchical structure of the Church has also faced criticism and scrutiny throughout its history. Critics argue that the concentration of power within the hierarchy can lead to abuses of authority and the silencing of dissenting voices. The top-down nature of decision-making within the Church has at times hindered transparency and accountability, allowing for the perpetuation of misconduct and corruption.

The Church's involvement in politics and its influence on governance.

Throughout history, the Catholic Church has wielded significant influence in the realm of politics and governance. This involvement in political affairs has allowed the Church to shape the course of nations, influence policies, and exert control over the lives of millions of people.

The Church's role in politics can be traced back to the early days of Christianity when the Roman Empire was the dominant power. Despite facing persecution, the early Christian community sought to spread its beliefs and gain acceptance within the existing political and social structures. With the conversion of Emperor Constantine to Christianity in the 4th century, Christianity became the official religion of the Roman Empire. This marked a turning point in the relationship between the Church and politics, as the Church became intertwined with the ruling powers.

Over the centuries, the Catholic Church continued to exert its influence on rulers and governments. By aligning with political leaders, the Church gained access to resources, protection, and support for its religious mission. Kings and emperors sought the blessing of the Church, cementing their legitimacy by aligning themselves with the divine authority represented by the religious institution. In turn, the Church was able to exercise power and influence over matters of governance, contributing to the shaping of laws, policies, and even the appointment of political leaders.

One significant way in which the Church influenced politics was through its role in education and the dissemination of knowledge. The Church was instrumental in developing the university system, which became a key institution for the education of scholars, theologians, and leaders. The Church controlled and funded many of the early universities, ensuring that the teachings of the Church were at the forefront of academic knowledge and shaping the intellectual landscape of Europe.

The Church's involvement in politics also extended to diplomatic matters and international relations. Through the papal diplomatic service, the Church played a vital role in fostering relationships between nations and mediating conflicts. Popes acted as intermediaries in negotiations, seeking to bring about peace and resolution in times of turmoil. Furthermore, the Church's influence was not limited to European politics; it extended to the colonization of the New World, as missionaries accompanied explorers and played a significant role in the establishment of European presence in the Americas.

The close relationship between the Church and politics has not been without controversy and conflict. Disputes between the Church and secular rulers, such as the Investiture Controversy in the Middle Ages, highlighted the tensions that arose when religious and political authorities clashed. The struggle for power and influence between the Church and secular rulers often led to political intrigue, power struggles, and even warfare.

In contemporary times, the Church's involvement in politics continues to be a subject of debate and contention. Discussions surrounding issues such as abortion, same-sex marriage, and social justice have seen the Church asserting its stance and advocating for particular policies. The Church's influence on political discourse remains significant, as its teachings and moral teachings shape the values and beliefs of many individuals and communities.

As we explore the history of abuse within the Catholic Church, we must also examine the ways in which its political entanglements have impacted the response to abuse cases and the accountability of the Church. The interplay between power, politics, and the protection of the institution has influenced the handling of abuse allegations and the quest for justice for survivors.

The development of the Church's doctrine and the enforcement of its teachings.

Throughout its history, the Catholic Church has engaged in the development of doctrinal teachings that serve as the foundation of its faith. These doctrines provide a framework for understanding and practicing the Catholic faith, shaping the lives of believers and guiding the Church's teachings and actions.

The development of Church doctrine has been a complex and dynamic process, influenced by theological debates, cultural shifts, and the challenges faced by the Church over the centuries. The doctrines of the Church are not static but have evolved and been refined through the efforts of theologians, bishops, and councils.

One significant milestone in the development of Church doctrine was the formulation of the Nicene Creed in the 4th century. This creed, agreed upon at the Council of Nicaea, articulated the basic beliefs of the Church, including the divinity of Jesus Christ and the nature of the Trinity. The Nicene Creed served as a unifying statement of faith and established a common ground for Christians across the Roman Empire.

Another key aspect of Church doctrine is the understanding and interpretation of Scripture. The interpretation of the Bible has always played a vital role in the formation of doctrine. The Church, through its various scholars and theologians, has sought to discern the meaning and significance of biblical texts, allowing for a deeper understanding of the faith and providing guidance to the faithful.

The authority to define and interpret doctrine lies with the Magisterium, the teaching authority of the Church. This authority is vested primarily in the Pope, who, in partnership with bishops and councils, has the responsibility to proclaim and clarify the teachings of the Church. The infallibility of the Pope on matters of faith and morals ensures the reliability and consistency of Church doctrine.

Enforcement of Church teachings has been carried out through various means throughout history. Excommunication, the most severe form of ecclesiastical penalty, was used to separate individuals or groups from the Church when they engaged in actions the Church deemed to be heretical or sinful. In addition to excommunication, the Church utilized penitential practices, such as fasting, confession, and pilgrimages, to encourage repentance and reconciliation with God.

The enforcement of Church doctrine has often been intertwined with the hierarchical structure of the Church, as bishops and priests play a crucial role in spreading and upholding Church teachings. Through sermons, catechesis, and pastoral care, they guide the faithful in understanding and living out the doctrines of the Church.

However, the enforcement of Church doctrine has not been without controversy and criticism. Instances of abuse of power, authoritarianism, and the silencing of dissenting views have marred the Church's history. The rigid enforcement of teachings without consideration for individual circumstances or ethical complexities has led to conflict and division within the Church and wider society.

As we explore the issue of abuse in the Catholic Church, we will examine how the Church's doctrinal teachings have intersected with the failures and shortcomings that allowed for the perpetration and cover-up of abuse. The tension between upholding doctrinal purity and addressing the needs and rights of survivors will be a central theme as we navigate the challenging terrain of hidden sins within the Church.

The controversies and criticisms surrounding the early Church's actions.

The early history of the Catholic Church was not without its controversies and criticisms. As the Church grew in power and influence, it faced scrutiny and faced challenges from both within and outside its ranks.

One of the earliest controversies that the Church faced was the division between the Eastern Orthodox Church and the Roman Catholic Church. This divide, known as the Great Schism, occurred in 1054 and led to the separation of the Eastern and Western branches of Christianity. The schism was characterized by theological disagreements, conflicts over church leadership, and differences in liturgical practices. The Great Schism remains a point of contention and division between the Catholic and Orthodox traditions to this day.

Another major controversy in the history of the early Church was the corruption and excesses of the medieval papacy. During this period, some popes engaged in acts of nepotism, simony (the buying and selling of church offices), and lived lavish lifestyles. These practices undermined the moral authority of the papacy and led to widespread criticism and calls for reform. The Church, in response to these criticisms, implemented reforms such as the Council of Trent in the 16th century, which sought to address issues of corruption and reaffirm the Church's teachings.

The Crusades, a series of military campaigns launched by the Catholic Church in the Middle Ages, also sparked controversy and division. While initially motivated by the goal of reclaiming holy sites in the Holy Land, the Crusades devolved into brutal conflicts that led to the loss of countless lives and strained relations between Christian and Muslim communities. The Crusades raised ethical questions and challenged the Church's commitment to peace and reconciliation.

Moreover, the Inquisition, a tribunal established by the Church to combat heresy, became notorious for its methods of interrogation and persecution. The Inquisition sought to root out individuals deemed to be dissenting from Church teachings, often using torture and violence to extract confessions. The Inquisition has been widely criticized for its human rights abuses and the suppression of intellectual freedom.

As the Catholic Church wielded significant political power throughout history, it also drew criticism for its involvement in politics, which at times led to conflict and the abuse of power. Instances of political intrigue, the accumulation of wealth, and the use of religious authority to control and manipulate rulers tarnished the reputation of the Church.

These controversies and criticisms surrounding the early Church's actions highlight the complexities and challenges the Church faced in its quest for power, influence, and the spread of the Christian faith. While the Church has made efforts to address these historical issues and implement reforms, these controversies serve as reminders of the Church's humanness and the need for ongoing introspection and accountability.

The Catholic Church's Influence on Society

The role of the Catholic Church in shaping social norms and values.

The role of the Catholic Church in shaping social norms and values cannot be understated. For centuries, the Church has held significant influence over the behaviors and attitudes of its followers. Through its teachings and moral guidelines, the Church has sought to guide individuals in leading virtuous lives and contributing to the well-being of society as a whole.

One of the ways in which the Catholic Church has exerted its influence is through its teachings on morality and ethics. The Church has provided a framework for understanding right from wrong, and its teachings on issues such as abortion, contraception, and marriage have shaped the moral landscape of society. By upholding certain values and condemning certain behaviors, the Church has influenced the choices and actions of its adherents.

Furthermore, the Catholic Church has played a crucial role in the development of education. Historically, the Church has been a major provider of education, establishing schools and universities that have shaped the minds of countless individuals. Through its emphasis on scholarship and intellectual pursuit, the Church has fostered a tradition of learning that has had a lasting impact on society. The Church's support for education has also empowered individuals, enabling them to pursue careers and contribute to their communities.

In addition to its influence on education, the Catholic Church has also made significant contributions to art, architecture, and cultural expressions. From the grand cathedrals of Europe to the intricate artwork found within them, the Church has been a patron of the arts throughout history. Through its support for artists and the creation of masterpieces, the Church has enriched society with beauty and inspiration. The cultural impact of the Church's patronage can still be seen today, as many works of art and architecture continue to captivate audiences.

The Church's impact on education and the dissemination of knowledge.

The Catholic Church's impact on education and the dissemination of knowledge has been profound. Throughout history, the Church has been a driving force behind the establishment of schools, universities, and educational institutions. The Church's commitment to the pursuit of knowledge and intellectual development has left an indelible mark on the education systems of many countries.

In the Middle Ages, the Catholic Church played a crucial role in the preservation and transmission of knowledge. Monastic orders, such as the Benedictines, dedicated themselves to copying and preserving ancient manuscripts, ensuring that the wisdom of the past was not lost to time. Monastic libraries became centers of learning where scholars could access a wealth of knowledge on a wide range of subjects.

During the Renaissance, the Church's patronage of scholars and artists contributed to a renewed interest in the humanities, sciences, and other fields of study. The Church sponsored the education of many renowned thinkers and supported the dissemination of their findings. This intellectual flourishing led to significant advancements in various disciplines, including philosophy, theology, mathematics, and astronomy.

In more recent times, the Catholic Church continues to be involved in education through the establishment and administration of schools. Catholic schools have a long-standing tradition of providing quality education, often emphasizing not only academic excellence but also the development of character and moral values. Catholic educational institutions seek to cultivate well-rounded individuals who are not only knowledgeable but also virtuous and socially conscious.

The Church's impact on education, however, has not been without controversy. In some instances, the Church's influence over curriculum and the inclusion of religious teachings in schools has faced criticism. There have also been instances of abuse and misconduct within Catholic educational institutions, which have called into question the Church's commitment to the welfare and safety of students.

The Church's role in promoting art, architecture, and cultural expressions.

The Catholic Church's role in promoting art, architecture, and cultural expressions has left an indelible mark on the world. Throughout history, the Church has been a patron of the arts, supporting and inspiring artists to create magnificent works that reflect the beauty and grandeur of the divine.

One of the most prominent ways in which the Church has influenced art is through the creation of sacred spaces. Cathedrals, basilicas, and churches stand as architectural masterpieces, showcasing the ingenuity and craftsmanship of the human spirit. These awe-inspiring structures, with their towering spires, intricate stained glass windows, and ornate sculptures, serve as a testament to the religious devotion and artistic prowess of those who built them.

The Church has not only supported the construction of grand architectural wonders but has also encouraged the creation of art that evokes spiritual contemplation and reverence. Religious paintings, sculptures, and mosaics have adorned the walls of churches and cathedrals, conveying the stories and teachings of the Bible and inviting worshippers to engage with the divine through artistic expression. These artistic creations have not only enriched the worship experience but have also contributed to the cultural heritage of communities worldwide.

Moreover, the Catholic Church's patronage has extended beyond the visual arts to include music, literature, and performing arts. Church hymns, oratorios, and Gregorian chants have enriched religious ceremonies and rituals, carrying the faithful on an emotional and spiritual journey. Many of the world's greatest composers, from Johann Sebastian Bach to Wolfgang Amadeus Mozart, created masterpieces inspired by their deep faith and influenced by the rich musical traditions of the Church.

In the realm of literature, the Church has been a source of inspiration for countless writers and poets. Religious themes and biblical stories have inspired timeless works, offering moral guidance, spiritual reflections, and narratives that resonate with readers across generations. The works of literary giants such as Dante Alighieri, John Milton, and Fyodor Dostoevsky bear the marks of their religious convictions and demonstrate the enduring power of religious storytelling.

The Church's support for the arts and cultural expressions has not been without its controversies. Throughout history, there have been instances of censorship and the suppression of artistic expressions deemed contrary to the teachings of the Church. Critics have also argued that the Church's influence on art has limited artistic freedom and expression.

The Church's influence on morality, ethics, and individual behavior.

The Catholic Church's influence on morality, ethics, and individual behavior has been extensive, shaping the values and ethical frameworks of its followers. Through its teachings and doctrines, the Church has provided guidance on how individuals should live their lives, offering moral principles and ethical guidelines to navigate the complexities of the world.

One of the key aspects of the Church's influence on morality is its emphasis on the dignity and sanctity of human life. The Church teaches that every human being is created in the image of God and possesses inherent worth and dignity. This belief forms the foundation for the Church's stance on issues such as abortion, euthanasia, and the death penalty, where it advocates for the protection of human life from conception to natural death.

Additionally, the Catholic Church's teachings on personal ethics emphasize the importance of virtues such as honesty, integrity, compassion, and selflessness. The Church encourages its followers to cultivate these virtues in their personal and professional lives, guiding them towards virtuous behavior and encouraging them to make choices that benefit others and contribute to the common good.

The Church's influence on individual behavior extends beyond personal virtues and extends to relationships and social interactions. For example, the Church places great emphasis on the institution of marriage and the importance of committed, faithful relationships. It provides guidance on issues such as divorce, contraception, and same-sex relationships, offering a moral framework for individuals to navigate these complex facets of human life.

Moreover, the Catholic Church's teachings on social justice and the preferential option for the poor have shaped its followers' attitudes towards philanthropy, charity, and social responsibility. The Church encourages its followers to care for the less fortunate and to actively work towards alleviating poverty, promoting equality, and advocating for justice in society.

While the Church's teachings on morality and ethics have provided a moral compass for its followers, they have not been without controversy and criticism. Some argue that the Church's conservative stance on certain social issues has been at odds with societal changes and advancements. Others question the Church's credibility in light of historical and recent scandals, which have raised concerns about hypocrisy and moral lapses within its own ranks.

The Church's involvement in charitable activities and social welfare.

The Catholic Church's involvement in charitable activities and social welfare has played a significant role in addressing the needs of communities and promoting social justice. Throughout history, the Church has been at the forefront of providing assistance to the marginalized, the poor, and the vulnerable, embodying the principles of compassion, altruism, and solidarity.

One of the key ways in which the Church has contributed to charitable activities is through the establishment of organizations and institutions dedicated to helping those in need. From orphanages and hospitals to homeless shelters and relief agencies, the Church has created a wide range of charitable institutions that provide vital services to individuals and communities. These initiatives seek to alleviate suffering, address basic needs, and empower individuals to thrive.

The Catholic Church's commitment to social welfare extends beyond direct assistance to encompass advocacy and social justice initiatives. The Church has been a vocal advocate for the rights of the oppressed, the marginalized, and the voiceless. It has championed causes such as human rights, environmental stewardship, and the eradication of poverty. The Church's teachings on social justice, rooted in the Gospel's call for love and solidarity, has inspired movements and initiatives focused on addressing systemic injustice and inequality.

Furthermore, the Catholic Church's engagement in charitable activities extends globally. Through international aid organizations and missionary work, the Church has reached out to communities in need across different continents. Its efforts in providing humanitarian aid, disaster relief, and development assistance have made a tangible difference in improving the lives of countless individuals and communities.

However, the Church's involvement in charitable activities has not been without challenges and controversies. There have been instances where the Church has faced criticism for mismanagement of funds, lack of transparency, and questions about the effectiveness of its initiatives. Additionally, debates have arisen regarding the compatibility of some of the Church's teachings with modern understandings of human rights and social justice.

The Church's reactions and responses to societal changes and challenges.

The Catholic Church's reactions and responses to societal changes and challenges have shaped its role and influence in contemporary times. As the world has evolved, the Church has faced various external and internal pressures that have necessitated a reassessment of its teachings, practices, and engagement with the wider society.

One of the notable reactions of the Church has been its response to scientific advancements. Throughout history, the Church has grappled with navigating the intersection of faith and reason, particularly in areas such as cosmology, evolution, and medical ethics. While there have been instances of tension and conflict, the Church has increasingly recognized the importance of dialogue and engagement with scientific knowledge. Today, many Catholic scholars and theologians actively explore the compatibility between faith and science, acknowledging the potential for mutual enrichment.

The Catholic Church has also responded to changing societal attitudes and values, particularly regarding issues of gender, sexuality, and human rights. In recent decades, there have been debates and discussions within the Church on topics such as women's roles within the institution, LGBTQ+ rights, and the inclusion of diverse voices. The Church's responses to these issues have varied, reflecting a balance between tradition and adaptation to the changing social landscape.

Furthermore, the Catholic Church has faced and addressed internal challenges related to its own institutional hierarchy and governance. The revelation of abuses and misconduct within the clergy has prompted the Church to confront the need for transparency, accountability, and structural reforms. Efforts have been made to address the systemic issues that allowed such abuses to persist, including the establishment of safeguarding mechanisms, enhanced training, and a greater emphasis on the protection of victims.

The Church's response to these societal changes and challenges has not occurred without tension and controversy. Different factions within the Church often hold diverging views and interpretations, leading to internal debates and disagreements. These dynamics reflect the complex nature of an institution that seeks to balance tradition, moral teachings, and the evolving needs of a changing world.

The Rise of Clerical Abuse

The historical factors contributing to the prevalence of abuse within the Catholic Church.

The roots of clerical abuse within the Catholic Church can be traced back to various historical factors that have influenced its prevalence. One significant factor is the hierarchical structure of the Church, which grants immense power and authority to clergy members. This concentration of power, combined with the reverence and trust placed in religious leaders, creates an environment where abuse can easily take place.

Additionally, the Church has historically emphasized notions of sin, guilt, and repentance, creating a culture that often prioritizes forgiveness over justice. This has allowed abusive individuals to evade accountability and continue their misconduct unchecked. Furthermore, the Church's long-standing practice of celibacy has been a source of controversy and debate, as it may contribute to a repressive environment that can manifest in harmful behaviors.

Another influential factor is the historical tolerance and cover-up of abuse cases within the Church. For many years, the Church has been plagued by a culture of secrecy and silence, where allegations of abuse were often swept under the rug to protect the institution's reputation. This complicity allowed abusive clergy members to continue their misconduct unabated, further perpetuating a cycle of abuse.

Moreover, societal attitudes and norms regarding sexuality and power dynamics have also played a role in enabling clerical abuse. The Church, as an influential institution, has been subject to social and cultural pressures that shape its response to abuse cases. In some instances, societal expectations of unquestioned respect for religious authorities have created an environment where victims may be dismissed or disbelieved when they come forward with allegations of abuse.

It is important to acknowledge that these historical factors are not excuses for the abuse that has taken place within the Catholic Church, but rather provide an understanding of the broader context in which the issue has emerged. By recognizing and addressing these historical factors, the Church can begin to take meaningful steps towards preventing future instances of abuse and fostering a culture of safety and accountability within its ranks.

The abuse of power by clergy and the consequences for victims.

Within the Catholic Church, the abuse of power by clergy members has been a distressing reality that has left a devastating impact on the lives of countless victims. The hierarchical structure of the Church has granted significant authority to clergy, making them figures of trust and reverence. However, some individuals within this position of power have used their authority to exploit vulnerable individuals, particularly children and young people.

The consequences for victims of clerical abuse are far-reaching and profound. The immediate impact often includes severe emotional and psychological trauma, ranging from feelings of shame, guilt, and betrayal to depression, anxiety, and even suicidal tendencies. These victims are left with deep scars that can affect them for the rest of their lives. The violation of trust by someone who was supposed to guide and protect them can shatter their sense of security and belief in the goodness of others.

Furthermore, the long-term effects of clerical abuse extend beyond the individual victims themselves. Families and communities are also profoundly affected, as their trust in the Church and its clergy is shattered. The ripple effects of abuse reach far and wide, creating a sense of disillusionment and eroding the fabric of faith and belief in the institution that was once held sacred.

It is important to acknowledge that the consequences of clerical abuse are not limited to the immediate victims. Society as a whole suffers when the integrity of religious institutions is compromised. The erosion of trust in the Church has broader implications, as many individuals may question their own faith, their engagement with religion, and their ability to place trust in religious authorities. This loss of trust affects not only the Catholic Church but also other religious institutions, as it raises concerns about the potential for similar abuse in other contexts.

Addressing and preventing clerical abuse requires a comprehensive effort that involves both the Church and wider society. The recognition and validation of victims' experiences, as well as providing them with the necessary support and resources, are essential steps towards healing and justice. Holding perpetrators accountable through legal and ethical systems is crucial to prevent future abuse and to ensure that the vulnerable within the Church are protected.

By shedding light on the abuse of power within the Catholic Church and its consequences, we can collectively work towards a safer and more accountable institution�one that upholds the principles of justice, compassion, and the well-being of all its members.

The culture of secrecy and silence within the Church that allowed abuse to persist.

One of the most disturbing aspects of clerical abuse within the Catholic Church is the prevalent culture of secrecy and silence that cultivated an environment in which abuse could persist unchecked. For years, the Church has been characterized by a reluctance to address allegations of abuse openly and honestly.

This culture of secrecy was perpetuated by several factors. First and foremost, there existed a widespread fear of tarnishing the reputation of the Church. The Church, as an institution that holds great influence and moral authority, was often more concerned with protecting itself from scandal than with addressing the needs and concerns of victims. This prioritization of reputation over the well-being of individuals allowed abuse to flourish behind closed doors.

Furthermore, the Church's hierarchical structure and its emphasis on obedience and loyalty likely contributed to the culture of silence. Clergy members were discouraged from questioning or challenging their superiors, including those who were involved in or aware of abuse. The fear of retribution, professional consequences, or even excommunication silenced many who may have otherwise spoken out.

The lack of transparency and accountability within the Church further perpetuated the culture of secrecy. Cases of abuse were often handled internally, outside the purview of civil authorities or independent oversight. This meant that perpetrators could continue their abuse with impunity, while victims were left without proper recourse. The absence of clear, consistent reporting and investigation protocols enabled the protection of abusers instead of the protection of the vulnerable.

Additionally, the Church's teachings and doctrines on forgiveness and redemption may have inadvertently contributed to the culture of secrecy. The emphasis on granting absolution and offering second chances can be misapplied in cases of abuse, leading some to believe that forgiveness absolves abusers from facing the consequences of their actions. This misinterpretation perpetuated a cycle of silence and allowed abusers to remain within the Church, potentially putting more individuals at risk.

It is crucial for the Catholic Church to confront and dismantle this culture of secrecy and silence. Transparency, accountability, and a commitment to the safety and well-being of its members should be at the forefront of its actions. By creating an environment in which survivors feel empowered to share their experiences and abusers are held accountable, the Church can begin to restore trust, promote healing, and prevent further instances of abuse.

The psychological and emotional impacts of abuse on survivors.

Clerical abuse within the Catholic Church has caused profound psychological and emotional impacts on survivors. The traumatic experiences endured by victims can have long-lasting effects that permeate various aspects of their lives.

First and foremost, survivors of clerical abuse often experience intense feelings of shame, guilt, and self-blame. They may question their own worth and struggle with a sense of powerlessness and betrayal. The violation of trust by someone who was supposed to represent moral authority and spiritual guidance creates a profound sense of confusion and betrayal. These feelings can lead to a loss of self-esteem and a struggle to establish healthy relationships and boundaries.

Survivors of abuse frequently suffer from a range of mental health issues, including depression, anxiety, post-traumatic stress disorder (PTSD), and suicidal thoughts. The lingering trauma can manifest in flashbacks, nightmares, and an overwhelming sense of fear and vulnerability. Daily life can become a coping mechanism, as survivors navigate through triggers and attempts to regain a sense of normalcy.

Moreover, the impacts of abuse extend beyond the psychological realm. Survivors often face physical health consequences as well, as the stress and trauma can take a toll on their overall well-being. The internalization of trauma can manifest in various physical symptoms, such as chronic pain, sleep disturbances, and compromised immune systems. The cumulative effects of abuse can lead to long-term health issues that require ongoing medical attention and care.

The road to healing for survivors of clerical abuse is challenging and complex. It requires a comprehensive and compassionate approach that addresses their psychological, emotional, and physical needs. Therapy, support groups, and survivor-centered programs can play a crucial role in helping survivors navigate through their trauma, process their experiences, and rebuild their lives. It is also essential for the Church to acknowledge and take responsibility for the harm inflicted, providing appropriate support, resources, and avenues for justice.

By recognizing the profound psychological and emotional impacts of abuse on survivors, society can better understand the urgency and necessity of preventing future instances of clerical abuse. It is a collective responsibility to create a safe and nurturing environment where individuals can seek solace, heal from past traumas, and rebuild their lives with dignity and resilience.

The complicity of higher-ranking clergy in covering up abuse cases.

One of the most distressing aspects of clerical abuse within the Catholic Church is the complicity of higher-ranking clergy in covering up abuse cases. This complicity has perpetuated a culture of impunity, allowing abusers to continue their actions while victims have been denied justice and support.

In many instances, reports of abuse were met with a concerted effort to protect the reputation of the Church rather than prioritize the safety and well-being of victims. This complicity often involved the deliberate concealment of evidence, the intimidation of victims and witnesses, and the reassignment of abusive clergy members to different parishes, allowing them to prey on new victims.

The motivations behind this complicity are multifaceted. Some high-ranking clergy may have been driven by a desire to maintain the image of the Church as a moral authority, fearing that public acknowledgment of abuse would undermine the faith of believers and weaken the influence of the institution. Others may have been concerned about potential legal and financial consequences that could arise from public exposure of abuse cases. The preservation of power, reputation, and institutional stability took precedence over the protection of victims.

Furthermore, the hierarchical structure of the Church played a significant role in enabling the complicity of higher-ranking clergy. The obedience and loyalty expected from lower-ranking clergy and the strict top-down decision-making process made it easier for those in positions of power to control the narrative surrounding abuse allegations. Fear of retribution and professional consequences deterred many within the Church from challenging the actions of their superiors and brought about a culture of silence.

The complicity of higher-ranking clergy in covering up abuse cases has caused immeasurable harm to victims and eroded trust within the Catholic Church. It has created a pervasive culture of secrecy and denial that has perpetuated the cycle of abuse and allowed abusers to operate with impunity. The exposure of these cover-ups has led to a loss of faith among believers and a growing demand for accountability and transparency within the Church.

To address this issue, it is essential for the Church to confront its history of cover-ups and actively work towards a culture of transparency and accountability. This includes holding responsible parties accountable, implementing robust reporting and investigation protocols, and ensuring that survivors of abuse receive the support and justice they deserve. By doing so, the Church can begin to restore trust and work towards preventing future instances of clerical abuse.

The failure of Church institutions to properly address and prevent abuse.

The failure of church institutions to properly address and prevent clerical abuse has been a profound disappointment for both believers and society at large. Despite the numerous cases that have come to light, many within the Catholic Church have been slow to acknowledge the extent of the problem and take decisive action to protect the vulnerable and hold abusers accountable.

One of the key failures of church institutions has been the inadequate response to allegations of abuse. In many cases, reports were met with skepticism, dismissal, or even victim-blaming. Victims were often discouraged from pursuing legal action or seeking justice, leaving them without proper avenues for recourse. This lack of support and validation only exacerbated their trauma and perpetuated a cycle of silence and complicity.

Furthermore, the lack of robust prevention measures has also contributed to the persistence of abuse within the Church. The failure to implement comprehensive protocols for screening and vetting clergy members allowed individuals with a history of abuse or potential for misconduct to enter and remain within the priesthood. The absence of thorough background checks, professional evaluations, and ongoing supervision enabled abusers to continue their harmful behavior while evading detection.

The hierarchical structure of the Church also played a role in impeding the prevention and proper handling of abuse cases. The concentration of power and decision-making authority in the hands of a select few allowed for the manipulation and cover-up of abuse allegations. Decisions concerning investigations, reporting, and disciplinary actions were often made behind closed doors, without the necessary transparency or accountability.

To address these failures, the Catholic Church must undergo a fundamental and systemic transformation. This includes implementing clear and effective reporting mechanisms for abuse allegations, ensuring that all cases are promptly referred to civil authorities, and cooperating fully with external investigations. The development and enforcement of rigorous prevention measures, such as comprehensive training programs and strict background checks, are also critical to prevent future instances of abuse.

Additionally, there needs to be a cultural shift within the Church, promoting a genuine commitment to the safety and well-being of its members. This includes listening to survivors, providing them with the support and resources they need, and acknowledging the harm inflicted upon them. By prioritizing the needs of victims and implementing meaningful reforms, the Catholic Church can begin to rebuild trust and reclaim its moral authority.

The role of the Vatican and its response to the abuse crisis.

The Vatican, as the highest governing body of the Catholic Church, has played a crucial role in the response to the clerical abuse crisis. Its actions, or lack thereof, have had far-reaching consequences on both the Church's reputation and the lives of survivors.

Initially, the response of the Vatican to allegations of clerical abuse was characterized by denial, deflection, and a lack of accountability. Reports and evidence of abuse were often met with an inclination to protect the institution, rather than prioritize the well-being of victims. This response not only compounded the pain and suffering of survivors but also undermined public trust in the Church's ability to address the issue effectively.

In recent years, however, there have been efforts within the Vatican to address the abuse crisis more directly. The establishment of the Pontifical Commission for the Protection of Minors and the issuance of guidelines aimed at preventing abuse are steps in the right direction. Pope Francis has also taken measures to hold clergy accountable for their actions, urging bishops to be transparent and take concrete actions to address allegations.

Nonetheless, critics argue that more needs to be done. The Vatican's response is often criticized for being slow, lacking in transparency, and failing to effectively address the systemic issues that contributed to the crisis. Calls for greater accountability, including the removal of abusive clergy and those who covered up their actions, have been met with mixed results.

Furthermore, survivors and advocacy groups have emphasized the need for a zero-tolerance policy towards abuse, along with comprehensive measures to ensure proper reporting, investigation, and support networks. They argue that only through genuine systemic change and a commitment to transparency and justice can the Vatican regain the trust and credibility it has lost.

The role of the Vatican in responding to the abuse crisis is pivotal. As the highest authority within the Church, its actions and policies set the tone for how the issue is addressed globally. By demonstrating a firm commitment to justice, transparency, and support for survivors, the Vatican can play a significant role in preventing future instances of abuse and fostering a culture of safety and accountability within the Catholic Church.

The global scope of clerical abuse and its impact on the Catholic Church's reputation.

The issue of clerical abuse extends far beyond the boundaries of a particular country or region, affecting the Catholic Church on a global scale. Reports and allegations of abuse have emerged from various parts of the world, revealing the widespread nature of this crisis and its profound impact on the Church's reputation.

Instances of clerical abuse have been documented in countries across continents, including North America, Europe, Latin America, Africa, and Asia. The sheer scope of these cases demonstrates that the problem is not confined to a few isolated incidents but is indicative of deeper systemic issues within the Church.

The global nature of the crisis has resulted in a significant erosion of trust in the Catholic Church. The revelations of abuse, cover-ups, and failures to address the issue have shaken the faith and confidence of believers, as well as the general public. Repeated instances of abuse and the subsequent mishandling of cases have led many to question the credibility and moral authority of the Church as an institution.

Moreover, the impact of the abuse crisis goes beyond the reputation of the Church itself. It has damaged the relationship between the Church and society, as well as with other religious institutions. Interfaith dialogue and ecumenical efforts may be strained due to the loss of trust and credibility caused by the abuse scandal. The Church's ability to engage with various social and political issues may also be compromised, as its moral authority is called into question.

To address this global crisis, it is essential for the Catholic Church to take substantive action on multiple fronts. This includes implementing robust prevention measures, ensuring the proper handling of abuse allegations, and holding accountable both the abusers and those who enabled them. Dedicated efforts are needed to provide support and justice to survivors, rebuild trust, and regain the Church's moral standing.

By acknowledging the global scope of the issue and taking decisive action, the Catholic Church can begin the process of healing, reconciliation, and reform. It is only through these collective efforts that the Church can work towards the prevention of future abuse and the restoration of its reputation as a force for compassion, justice, and spiritual guidance.The global scope of the clerical abuse crisis within the Catholic Church has had far-reaching consequences, both for the Church itself and for the lives of survivors. Reports and allegations of abuse have emerged from various parts of the world, revealing the widespread nature of this crisis and its profound impact on the Church's reputation.

Instances of clerical abuse have been documented in countries across continents, including North America, Europe, Latin America, Africa, and Asia. The sheer scope of these cases demonstrates that the problem is not confined to a few isolated incidents but is indicative of deeper systemic issues within the Church.

The global nature of the crisis has resulted in a significant erosion of trust in the Catholic Church. The revelations of abuse, cover-ups, and failures to address the issue have shaken the faith and confidence of believers, as well as the general public. Repeated instances of abuse and the subsequent mishandling of cases have led many to question the credibility and moral authority of the Church as an institution.

Moreover, the impact of the abuse crisis goes beyond the reputation of the Church itself. It has damaged the relationship between the Church and society, as well as with other religious institutions. Interfaith dialogue and ecumenical efforts may be strained due to the loss of trust and credibility caused by the abuse scandal. The Church's ability to engage with various social and political issues may also be compromised, as its moral authority is called into question.

To address this global crisis, it is essential for the Catholic Church to take substantive action on multiple fronts. This includes implementing robust prevention measures, ensuring the proper handling of abuse allegations, and holding accountable both the abusers and those who enabled them. Dedicated efforts are needed to provide support and justice to survivors, rebuild trust, and regain the Church's moral standing.

By acknowledging the global scope of the issue and taking decisive action, the Catholic Church can begin the process of healing, reconciliation, and reform. It is only through these collective efforts that the Church can work towards the prevention of future abuse and the restoration of its reputation as a force for compassion, justice, and spiritual guidance.

The Church's Response to the Abuse Crisis

The evolution of the Church's policies and protocols in response to abuse.

In the wake of mounting allegations, the Catholic Church was forced to confront the undeniable reality of clerical abuse within its ranks. The early response was often haphazard and lacking in consistency, with individual dioceses and bishops handling cases in their own ways. However, as the crisis continued to unfold and public outcry grew louder, the Church was compelled to develop more comprehensive policies and protocols to address the issue. These measures aimed to ensure a uniform and standardized approach to handling abuse allegations, as well as to provide support for survivors and hold perpetrators accountable.

One of the key developments in the Church's response was the establishment of guidelines for the handling of abuse cases. These guidelines laid out the procedures for reporting allegations, conducting investigations, and implementing disciplinary actions. They sought to strike a balance between the rights of the accused and the need to protect the vulnerable, while also preserving the Church's reputation. These guidelines were informed by the input of legal experts, mental health professionals, and survivors themselves, in an effort to create a more victim-centered approach.

Another significant aspect of the Church's response was the establishment of centralized investigative bodies and internal review processes. These bodies were tasked with thoroughly examining allegations of abuse and determining their veracity. They operated independently of local dioceses and were granted the authority to make recommendations for further action, including the removal of offending clergy from their positions. By centralizing the investigative process, the Church aimed to ensure a more consistent and objective assessment of abuse allegations.

Additionally, the Church recognized the need for proactive measures to prevent abuse from occurring in the first place. Safeguarding measures were implemented to screen and train clergy, providing them with the necessary knowledge and tools to identify and prevent abusive behavior. This included comprehensive background checks, psychological evaluations, and ongoing education on appropriate boundaries and ethical conduct. The goal was to create an environment where abuse was less likely to occur and where potential victims felt safe and protected.

However, the Church's response to the abuse crisis has not been without its challenges and controversies. The implementation of these measures has been inconsistent across different regions, with some dioceses demonstrating a greater commitment to transparency and accountability than others. There have also been criticisms of the lack of external oversight and the perceived insularity of the Church's investigative processes. Moreover, questions have been raised about the adequacy of the disciplinary actions taken against offending clergy, with some arguing that more punitive measures should be employed to deter future abuse.

Despite these challenges, the Church's response to the abuse crisis has undoubtedly marked a significant shift in its approach to addressing misconduct within its ranks. The development of policies, the establishment of investigative bodies, and the implementation of safeguarding measures demonstrate a growing recognition of the need for transparency, accountability, and justice. However, there is still considerable work to be done to ensure that these measures are consistently enforced and that the Church can rebuild trust and regain credibility.

The establishment of investigative bodies and internal review processes.

Recognizing the seriousness of the abuse crisis and the need for an independent and thorough investigation into allegations of misconduct, the Catholic Church established specialized investigative bodies and internal review processes. These entities were designed to ensure that allegations of abuse were handled professionally, impartially, and in accordance with the principles of due process.

One notable example is the formation of review boards consisting of professionals from diverse backgrounds, such as law enforcement, psychology, social work, and legal expertise. These review boards were tasked with evaluating abuse allegations and making informed recommendations to ecclesiastical authorities. By including individuals with expertise in relevant fields outside of the Church hierarchy, the aim was to ensure an unbiased and objective assessment of the allegations.

The review boards were given the authority to conduct thorough investigations into allegations of abuse. This involved gathering evidence, interviewing witnesses, and reviewing relevant documentation. The investigative process was intended to be transparent and comprehensive, allowing for a fair evaluation of the allegations and the determination of appropriate disciplinary actions if necessary.

In addition to the external review boards, the Catholic Church also established internal review processes within dioceses and religious orders. These processes involved the appointment of qualified individuals, often called victims' advocates or ombudspersons, who were responsible for receiving and addressing accusations of abuse in a sensitive and empathetic manner. These individuals played a crucial role in providing support to survivors and guiding them through the often complex and emotionally challenging process of reporting abuse.

Furthermore, the establishment of internal review processes aimed to encourage a culture of accountability within the Church. By creating channels for reporting and investigating abuse allegations, the Church sought to send a clear message that misconduct would not be tolerated and that survivors would be heard and supported. These internal review processes were intended to complement the work of external investigative bodies, ensuring that no allegations slipped through the cracks and that accountability was upheld.

However, despite the establishment of these investigative bodies and internal review processes, the Church has faced criticism for the lack of transparency and independence in some cases. There have been instances where the Church was accused of protecting its own interests by concealing information or failing to fully cooperate with external investigations. These controversies have highlighted the need for greater external oversight and an enhanced commitment to transparency to restore public trust in the Church's ability to effectively address the abuse crisis.

In summary, the creation of specialized investigative bodies and internal review processes within the Catholic Church marked an important step towards addressing the issue of abuse. These entities were aimed at ensuring independent and unbiased investigations into allegations, providing support to survivors, and holding perpetrators accountable. However, ongoing challenges remain in terms of transparency and external oversight, necessitating further reforms to strengthen the Church's response to the abuse crisis.

The implementation of safeguarding measures and

training for clergy.

In addition to establishing investigative bodies and internal review processes, the Catholic Church recognized the importance of prevention and the need for comprehensive safeguarding measures and training for clergy. The implementation of these measures aimed to create a culture of awareness, transparency, and accountability within the Church, with the goal of preventing future instances of abuse.

Safeguarding measures encompass a range of policies and protocols designed to ensure the safety and well-being of vulnerable individuals, particularly children and vulnerable adults, who may come into contact with clergy members. These measures include thorough background checks for all individuals seeking ordination or working within the Church, as well as those involved in ministry with vulnerable populations. Background checks help identify any past instances of misconduct or criminal behavior and serve as an important preventive measure.

Furthermore, the Catholic Church has recognized the importance of ongoing education and training for clergy on abuse prevention. This includes providing comprehensive training programs focused on recognizing signs of abuse, appropriate boundaries, and ethical conduct. Such training helps equip clergy members with the knowledge and skills necessary to identify and address situations that may lead to abuse, ensuring the safety and well-being of those under their care.

In addition, the Church has also emphasized the importance of mandatory reporting of abuse allegations to civil authorities, in line with local laws and regulations. This serves to ensure that law enforcement agencies are involved in investigating such cases, promoting transparency and accountability. By cooperating with civil authorities, the Church aims to demonstrate its commitment to addressing abuse and working collaboratively to protect vulnerable individuals.

Furthermore, the Church has implemented codes of conduct for clergy members, outlining the expected standards of behavior and the consequences for violations. These codes of conduct make it clear that any form of abuse, whether physical, emotional, or sexual, is strictly prohibited and will be met with disciplinary action.

The implementation of safeguarding measures and training for clergy is an ongoing process. The Catholic Church continues to refine and enhance these measures in response to new challenges and evolving best practices. It is also important to note that these efforts are not limited to the clergy alone but extend to all individuals involved in Church ministries and activities, including lay volunteers and employees.

While the implementation of these measures is a positive step forward, there have been criticisms of their effectiveness and consistency across dioceses. Some argue that there is a need for greater oversight and accountability, as well as ensuring that these measures are consistently enforced and updated to reflect changing societal norms and expectations.

In conclusion, the Catholic Church has implemented safeguarding measures and training programs aimed at preventing abuse and promoting a culture of safety within its ranks. These measures include thorough background checks, education and training programs, mandatory reporting, and codes of conduct. While there are challenges to overcome, the Church's commitment to addressing abuse and protecting vulnerable individuals is evident in the ongoing development and implementation of these measures.

The Church's efforts to provide support for survivors of abuse.

Recognizing the profound impact that abuse can have on survivors, the Catholic Church has made efforts to provide support and healing services for those who have experienced abuse within the Church. These efforts are aimed at acknowledging the pain and suffering endured by survivors, and assisting them in their journey towards healing and recovery.

One important aspect of the Church's support for survivors is the establishment of dedicated victim assistance programs. These programs provide a range of services, such as counseling, therapy, and support groups, tailored to the specific needs of abuse survivors. Trained professionals, often from outside the Church, are available to offer emotional support, guidance, and resources to help survivors navigate the healing process.

In addition, the Church has taken steps to ensure that survivors are provided with options for seeking justice and redress. This includes the establishment of compensation funds, which provide financial restitution to survivors who have suffered abuse. These funds aim to acknowledge the harm inflicted upon survivors and provide them with a form of recognition and support.

Furthermore, the Church has made efforts to facilitate meaningful engagement and dialogue with survivors. Listening sessions, where survivors are given the opportunity to share their experiences and provide input on the Church's response to abuse, have been organized to ensure that their voices are heard. This engagement is crucial in shaping the Church's ongoing efforts to address the abuse crisis and to learn from the experiences and perspectives of survivors.

Moreover, the Catholic Church has sought to collaborate with outside organizations and experts in the field of abuse prevention and survivor support. Partnerships with established organizations, such as victim advocacy groups and mental health professionals, have helped to strengthen the Church's response and ensure the provision of high-quality support services. These collaborations bring in external expertise and help to foster a more comprehensive approach to survivor support.

While these efforts demonstrate a commitment to supporting survivors, the Church acknowledges that there is still much work to be done. Acknowledgment of past failures and sincere apologies to survivors have been important steps in the healing process. However, it is essential that the Church continue to listen, learn, and adapt its support services to meet the evolving needs of survivors.

In conclusion, the Catholic Church's efforts to provide support for survivors of abuse demonstrate a recognition of the profound harm caused by abuse within its ranks. The establishment of victim assistance programs, compensation funds, and meaningful engagement with survivors reflect a commitment to healing and justice. By collaborating with external organizations and continuously improving support services, the Church aims to ensure that survivors are not only heard but also provided with the necessary resources and care to aid in their healing journey.

The collaboration and accountability efforts between Church and civil authorities.

Addressing the abuse crisis within the Catholic Church has required collaboration and accountability between the Church and civil authorities. Recognizing the magnitude and complexity of the issue, the Church has sought to work hand in hand with government agencies and legal systems to ensure that offenders are held accountable and survivors' rights are protected.

One significant development in this regard has been the Church's commitment to cooperating with civil authorities in the investigation and prosecution of abuse cases. This collaboration involves sharing information and evidence with law enforcement agencies, as well as providing support to survivors in pursuing legal avenues of justice. By aligning with legal systems and actively participating in investigations, the Church aims to demonstrate its willingness to work within the confines of the law to address abuse.

In some instances, the Church has also established independent oversight committees or commissions, composed of individuals with legal expertise and experience in child protection. These committees are tasked with reviewing cases of abuse, ensuring that appropriate actions are taken within the framework of civil law, and preventing any interference or obstruction in the pursuit of justice. Their recommendations and findings can serve as a crucial source of accountability within the Church.

Additionally, the Church has implemented measures to strengthen background checks and reporting practices for clergy and members working with vulnerable populations. These measures are often developed in consultation with legal experts to ensure compliance with laws and regulations governing child protection. By aligning with legal requirements, the Church aims to further enhance accountability and prevent instances of abuse.

The collaborative efforts between the Church and civil authorities have also extended to the sharing of best practices and information. This exchange of knowledge helps to ensure that the Church is informed about legal developments, emerging trends, and effective strategies in prevention and response to abuse. By learning from the experiences of other organizations and jurisdictions, the Church can continue to improve its practices and strengthen accountability.

However, it is important to note that collaboration with civil authorities can sometimes come with challenges. The Church's status as a religious institution, along with issues of jurisdiction and autonomy, can create complexities in the interface between Church and state. Navigating these complexities requires ongoing dialogue, mutual understanding, and a shared commitment to the protection of vulnerable individuals.

In conclusion, the collaborative efforts and accountability measures between the Catholic Church and civil authorities have been key in addressing the abuse crisis. By cooperating with law enforcement agencies, establishing oversight committees, and aligning with legal requirements, the Church aims to ensure that offenders are held accountable and survivors' rights are protected. Continued collaboration and information sharing will be crucial in the ongoing efforts to prevent abuse and foster accountability within the Catholic Church.

The ongoing challenges, controversies, and criticism of the Church's response.

Despite the efforts made by the Catholic Church to address the abuse crisis, there are ongoing challenges, controversies, and criticisms surrounding its response to these issues. These challenges highlight the need for continued improvement and vigilance in ensuring the safety and well-being of the faithful.

One persistent challenge is the lack of consistent implementation of safeguarding measures and protocols across different regions and within different dioceses. There are instances where allegations of abuse have been mishandled or not taken seriously, leading to ongoing pain and suffering for survivors. This inconsistency raises concerns about accountability and the effectiveness of the Church's response to abuse.

Controversies have also emerged regarding the perceived lack of transparency and accountability within the Church. Critics argue that the Church has often prioritized its own reputation and interests, sometimes at the expense of survivors and justice. Instances of cover-ups and the failure to report abuse to civil authorities have further eroded trust in the Church's ability to address the crisis effectively.

Moreover, there has been ongoing criticism of the Church's disciplinary actions and the perceived leniency towards offending clergy. Some survivors and advocates argue that more stringent measures, such as defrocking and criminal prosecution, should be applied to ensure that justice is served and to prevent further instances of abuse. The perceived lack of consequences for those responsible has fueled public distrust and skepticism towards the Church's commitment to change.

Furthermore, there is a need for the Church to address the underlying systemic issues that have allowed abuse to persist. This includes examining the culture of secrecy and silence, the power dynamics within the Church, and the roles and responsibilities of bishops and other higher-ranking clergy. Critics argue that true reform requires a comprehensive examination of these structural and cultural factors and the implementation of measures that address them.

It is important to recognize that the Catholic Church is not the only institution grappling with these issues. The abuse crisis has exposed deep-rooted problems within many organizations and societal structures. However, as a religious institution with significant influence and moral authority, the Catholic Church faces heightened scrutiny and expectations for meaningful change.

In response to these challenges and criticisms, there is an increasing call for greater external oversight and independent investigations into abuse allegations within the Church. Some argue that this would help to restore public trust and provide survivors with a sense of justice and closure. Additionally, continued collaboration between the Church and civil authorities is viewed as essential to ensuring transparency, accountability, and the protection of vulnerable individuals.

In conclusion, while the Catholic Church has made efforts to address the abuse crisis, ongoing challenges, controversies, and criticisms persist. Inconsistent implementation of safeguarding measures, issues of transparency and accountability, and calls for more stringent actions against offenders are among the key areas of concern. The Church must remain committed to continued improvement, accountability, and collaboration in order to heal the wounds of survivors and restore faith in its ability to prevent abuse in the future.

Lessons Learned and Steps Forward

The importance of transparency and accountability in preventing future abuse.

One of the key lessons that have emerged from the Catholic Church's abuse crisis is the critical importance of transparency and accountability in preventing future instances of abuse. The veil of secrecy that has shrouded many abuse cases has allowed perpetrators to continue their actions unchecked and has caused immeasurable harm to countless victims. To address this issue, the Church must prioritize transparency by creating clear and open channels for reporting abuse, ensuring that victims are heard and their voices are given the utmost importance.

Transparency also requires holding those responsible for abuse accountable for their actions. This includes not only the perpetrators themselves but also those within the Church hierarchy who have enabled or covered up these crimes. It is through holding individuals accountable that the Church can send a clear message that abuse will not be tolerated and that the safety and well-being of its members are paramount.

However, achieving transparency and accountability requires a comprehensive overhaul of the existing systems and structures within the Church. This includes the establishment of independent investigative bodies that are free from any potential conflicts of interest. These bodies should have the authority to conduct thorough investigations into allegations of abuse and to ensure that appropriate actions are taken based on their findings.

Additionally, the Church must be proactive in cooperating with civil authorities in the investigation and prosecution of abuse cases. Collaboration between Church and state can provide a more comprehensive and effective response to these crimes, ensuring that justice is served and that perpetrators are held accountable under the law.

By prioritizing transparency and accountability, the Catholic Church can take significant steps towards preventing future instances of abuse. It is through these measures that the Church can rebuild trust, restore its moral authority, and create a safe and secure environment for its members. However, it is crucial to acknowledge that achieving these goals will require continued dedication, vigilance, and a steadfast commitment to the well-being of all individuals within the Church community. Only by confronting the hidden sins of the past and actively working towards a better future can the Church truly heal and move forward.

The need for continuous education and training of clergy on abuse prevention.

In addition to transparency and accountability, another crucial step forward for the Catholic Church in preventing abuse is the need for continuous education and training of clergy on abuse prevention. It is imperative that those in positions of power within the Church are equipped with the knowledge and tools necessary to identify and address potential instances of abuse.

Education and training programs should focus on raising awareness about the dynamics of abuse, the signs to look out for, and the appropriate steps to take when suspicions arise. Clergy members must be educated on the impact of abuse on victims, the long-lasting trauma it causes, and the importance of providing support and validation to survivors.

Moreover, training programs should emphasize the significance of creating safe environments within the Church. This can include establishing clear boundaries, implementing robust safeguarding measures, and fostering a culture of openness and trust. By teaching clergy how to recognize and address potential risks, the Church can create a community that prioritizes the well-being and safety of its members, particularly the most vulnerable.

Continuous education and training should not be limited to new clergy members but should be an ongoing process throughout their careers. This ensures that clergy stay updated on the latest research, best practices, and techniques for preventing abuse. It is crucial to promote a culture of learning and growth within the Church, where clergy members are encouraged to continually improve their understanding of abuse prevention and intervention strategies.

Furthermore, collaboration with experts in the field of abuse prevention and victim support is vital. The Church should seek partnerships with organizations and professionals who specialize in addressing abuse, trauma, and the needs of survivors. By working with external experts, the Church can access the latest research, gain valuable insights, and ensure that its practices align with the best possible standards.

By investing in continuous education and training, the Catholic Church demonstrates its commitment to preventing abuse and creating a safer environment for its members. This proactive approach not only empowers clergy to take appropriate actions but also sends a clear message that the Church is dedicated to eradicating abuse and protecting the dignity and well-being of all individuals within its community.

The potential for the Catholic Church to rebuild trust and regain credibility.

After the extensive damage caused by the abuse crisis, one of the most critical steps forward for the Catholic Church is the potential to rebuild trust and regain credibility. Rebuilding trust is a complex and multifaceted process that requires sincere and consistent actions on the part of the Church.

First and foremost, the Church must demonstrate a genuine commitment to transparency and accountability, as discussed earlier. This includes being fully transparent about past abuses, acknowledging the pain caused to survivors, and taking decisive actions against those responsible. It also involves implementing robust safeguarding measures and establishing an environment where victims are encouraged to come forward and receive the support they need.

Additionally, the Church should actively engage with survivors and their advocates to listen to their experiences, acknowledge their pain, and work towards healing and justice. This requires a compassionate and empathetic approach, recognizing the immense courage it takes for survivors to come forward and share their stories. By genuinely listening to survivors and taking their concerns seriously, the Church can begin to rebuild trust and show its commitment to prioritizing the well-being of its members.

Furthermore, the Church must prioritize ongoing efforts to prevent future abuses. This includes continuously evaluating and improving its policies, practices, and training programs. By showcasing a sincere dedication to learning from past mistakes and implementing concrete measures to prevent abuse, the Church can begin to regain credibility in the eyes of its members and the wider public.

Importantly, the Church should also foster a culture of accountability, where those in positions of power are held responsible for their actions. This includes not only addressing cases of abuse but also tackling any instances of cover-ups or negligence. By holding individuals accountable, regardless of their rank or position within the Church hierarchy, the institution can demonstrate its commitment to justice and fairness.

Ultimately, rebuilding trust and regaining credibility is a long-term endeavor that requires unwavering commitment and consistency. It necessitates a holistic approach that addresses the underlying issues, implements robust preventative measures, and ensures justice for survivors. By facing the dark chapters of its history head-on and taking meaningful actions, the Catholic Church can gradually rebuild trust and work towards healing, reconciliation, and a renewed reputation as a moral authority in society.

Did you love *Saints and Sinners: The Untold Stories of Abuse in the catholic church*? Then you should read *The Dark Side of the Vatican*[1] by Sophia Fairview!

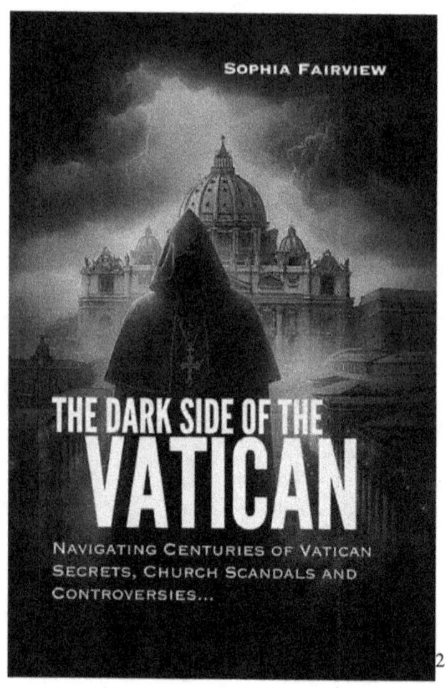

[2]

"Unveiling Shadows: The Dark side of the Vatican" is a gripping and meticulously researched exploration of the hidden facets of the Vatican's history, revealing the institution's darkest secrets and controversies. Delve into the shadows of one of the world's most powerful religious institutions and uncover the truth that has long been concealed.

---

1. https://books2read.com/u/mV26dA

2. https://books2read.com/u/mV26dA

In this eye-opening book, you will journey through the tumultuous history of the Vatican, from the establishment of the Papal Inquisition to the scandals that rocked the Church during World War II. Explore the lives of controversial figures like Pope Alexander VI, whose reign was marked by nepotism and corruption, and the brilliant scientist Galileo Galilei, who clashed with the Church's dogma.

"Unveiling Shadows" sheds light on the scandals that have plagued the Vatican, including the sexual abuse crisis that has shaken the faith of millions. Discover the stories of those who spoke out against abuse and faced the wrath of the Church's hierarchy.

This meticulously researched book also offers a timeline of significant events, biographies of key figures, and an in-depth examination of high-profile sexual abuse cases within the Church. It confronts the moral dilemmas faced by the Vatican, the role of secrecy in its operations, and the ongoing quest for justice and accountability.

"Unveiling Shadows" is a compelling and thought-provoking account that challenges the traditional narrative and delves deep into the heart of the Vatican's darkest moments. It is a must-read for anyone seeking to understand the complex history and controversies surrounding one of the world's most influential institutions.

www.ingramcontent.com/pod-product-compliance
Lightning Source LLC
Chambersburg PA
CBHW071500130726

47997CB00006B/2413